CLARINET

# THE BIG BOOK OF CHRISTMAS SONGS

Available for

FLUTE, CLARINET, ALTO SAX, TENOR SAX, TRUMPET, HORN, TROMBONE, VIOLIN, VIOLA, CELLO

T0039521

ISBN-13: 978-1-4234-1367-7

HAL•LEONARD® CORPORATION
7777 W. BLUEMOUND RD. P.O. BOX 13819 MILWAUKEE, WI 53213

5 A CAROLING WE GO
4 ALL I WANT FOR CHRISTMAS IS YOU
6 ALL MY HEART THIS NIGHT REJOICES
6 ALL THROUGH THE NIGHT
7 ANGELS FROM THE REALMS OF GLORY
7 ANGELS WE HAVE HEARD ON HIGH
8 AS LONG AS THERE'S CHRISTMAS
10 AS WITH GLADNESS MEN OF OLD
10 AULD LANG SYNE
10 AWAY IN A MANGER (KIRKPATRICK)
17 AWAY IN A MANGER (MURRAY)
14 BABY, IT'S COLD OUTSIDE
16 BECAUSE IT'S CHRISTMAS (FOR ALL THE CHILDREN)
18 BLUE CHRISTMAS
19 THE BOAR'S HEAD CAROL
11 BRAZILIAN SLEIGH BELLS
18 BREAK FORTH, O BEAUTEOUS, HEAVENLY LIGHT
20 BRING A TORCH, JEANNETTE, ISABELLA
19 C-H-R-I-S-T-M-A-S
20 CAROL OF THE BELLS
21 CAROL OF THE BIRDS
22 CAROLING, CAROLING
23 A CHILD IS BORN IN BETHLEHEM
22 THE CHIPMUNK SONG
23 CHRIST WAS BORN ON CHRISTMAS DAY
24 CHRISTMAS ALL ACROSS THE U.S.A.
25 CHRISTMAS IN DIXIE
28 CHRISTMAS IS
30 CHRISTMAS IS A-COMIN' (MAY GOD BLESS YOU)
26 CHRISTMAS IS ALL IN THE HEART
31 THE CHRISTMAS SONG (CHESTNUTS ROASTING ON AN OPEN FIRE)
28 CHRISTMAS STAR
29 CHRISTMAS TIME IS HERE
33 THE CHRISTMAS WALTZ
32 COLD DECEMBER NIGHTS
34 COME, THOU LONG-EXPECTED JESUS
34 COVENTRY CAROL
35 DANCE OF THE SUGAR PLUM FAIRY
35 DECK THE HALL
40 DING DONG! MERRILY ON HIGH!
36 DO THEY KNOW IT'S CHRISTMAS?
40 DO YOU HEAR WHAT I HEAR
38 DON'T SAVE IT ALL FOR CHRISTMAS DAY
41 FELIZ NAVIDAD
43 THE FIRST NOEL
43 THE FRIENDLY BEASTS
43 FROM HEAVEN ABOVE TO EARTH I COME
42 FROSTY THE SNOW MAN
48 FUM, FUM, FUM
44 THE GIFT
48 GO, TELL IT ON THE MOUNTAIN
49 GOD REST YE MERRY, GENTLEMEN
46 GOING HOME FOR CHRISTMAS
49 GOOD CHRISTIAN MEN, REJOICE
49 GOOD KING WENCESLAS
50 GRANDMA GOT RUN OVER BY A REINDEER
51 GRANDMA'S KILLER FRUITCAKE
52 THE GREATEST GIFT OF ALL
56 GREENWILLOW CHRISTMAS
54 GROWN-UP CHRISTMAS LIST
56 HAPPY CHRISTMAS, LITTLE FRIEND
58 HAPPY HANUKKAH, MY FRIEND (THE HANUKKAH SONG)
59 HAPPY HOLIDAY
62 HAPPY XMAS (WAR IS OVER)
60 HARD CANDY CHRISTMAS
53 HARK! THE HERALD ANGELS SING
60 HE
55 HE IS BORN, THE HOLY CHILD
61 HERE COMES SANTA CLAUS (RIGHT DOWN SANTA CLAUS LANE)
63 HERE WE COME A-WASSAILING
63 THE HOLLY AND THE IVY
66 A HOLLY JOLLY CHRISTMAS
64 (THERE'S NO PLACE LIKE) HOME FOR THE HOLIDAYS
65 HYMNE
66 I AM SO GLAD ON CHRISTMAS EVE
67 I HEARD THE BELLS ON CHRISTMAS DAY (CALKIN)
67 I HEARD THE BELLS ON CHRISTMAS DAY (MARKS)
68 I SAW MOMMY KISSING SANTA CLAUS
67 I SAW THREE SHIPS
68 I WONDER AS I WANDER
71 I'LL BE HOME FOR CHRISTMAS
69 I'M SPENDING CHRISTMAS WITH YOU
70 I'VE GOT MY LOVE TO KEEP ME WARM
71 IN THE BLEAK MIDWINTER
73 IT CAME UPON THE MIDNIGHT CLEAR
72 IT MUST HAVE BEEN THE MISTLETOE (OUR FIRST CHRISTMAS)
74 IT'S BEGINNING TO LOOK LIKE CHRISTMAS
76 IT'S CHRISTMAS TIME ALL OVER THE WORLD
75 IT'S JUST ANOTHER NEW YEAR'S EVE

78 JESU, JOY OF MAN'S DESIRING
77 JESUS HOLY, BORN SO LOWLY
82 JINGLE-BELL ROCK
80 JINGLE BELLS
80 JINGLE, JINGLE, JINGLE
81 JOLLY OLD ST. NICHOLAS
85 JOY TO THE WORLD
84 LAST CHRISTMAS
88 THE LAST MONTH OF THE YEAR (WHAT MONTH WAS JESUS BORN IN?)
87 LET IT SNOW! LET IT SNOW! LET IT SNOW!
83 LET'S HAVE AN OLD FASHIONED CHRISTMAS
88 LITTLE SAINT NICK
89 LO, HOW A ROSE E'ER BLOOMING
86 (EVERYBODY'S WAITIN' FOR) THE MAN WITH THE BAG
90 MARCH OF THE THREE KINGS
91 A MARSHMALLOW WORLD
92 MASTERS IN THIS HALL
92 MELE KALIKIMAKA
93 MERRY CHRISTMAS, BABY
94 MERRY CHRISTMAS, DARLING
95 MERRY CHRISTMAS, MERRY CHRISTMAS
97 THE MERRY CHRISTMAS POLKA
98 A MERRY, MERRY CHRISTMAS TO YOU
96 MISS YOU MOST AT CHRISTMAS TIME
98 MISTER SANTA
99 MISTLETOE AND HOLLY
100 THE MOST WONDERFUL DAY OF THE YEAR
102 THE MOST WONDERFUL TIME OF THE YEAR
103 MY FAVORITE THINGS
104 MY ONLY WISH THIS YEAR
101 THE NIGHT BEFORE CHRISTMAS SONG
106 NUTTIN' FOR CHRISTMAS
105 O CHRISTMAS TREE
106 O COME, ALL YE FAITHFUL
107 O COME, LITTLE CHILDREN
108 O COME, O COME IMMANUEL
109 O HOLY NIGHT
108 O LITTLE TOWN OF BETHLEHEM
108 O SANCTISSIMA
109 OF THE FATHER'S LOVE BEGOTTEN
110 OLD TOY TRAINS
110 ON CHRISTMAS NIGHT
113 ONCE IN ROYAL DAVID'S CITY
114 PAT-A-PAN (WILLIE, TAKE YOUR LITTLE DRUM)
112 PLEASE COME HOME FOR CHRISTMAS
111 PRETTY PAPER
114 RISE UP, SHEPHERD, AND FOLLOW
115 ROCKIN' AROUND THE CHRISTMAS TREE
116 RUDOLPH THE RED-NOSED REINDEER
117 SANTA BABY
120 SANTA, BRING MY BABY BACK (TO ME)
118 SANTA CLAUS IS BACK IN TOWN
118 SANTA CLAUS IS COMIN' TO TOWN
119 SHAKE ME I RATTLE (SQUEEZE ME I CRY)
121 SHEPHERDS, SHAKE OFF YOUR DROWSY SLEEP
122 SILENT NIGHT
121 SILVER AND GOLD
122 SILVER BELLS
123 SING WE NOW OF CHRISTMAS
123 SNOWFALL
125 SOME CHILDREN SEE HIM
124 SOME THINGS FOR CHRISTMAS (A SNAKE, SOME MICE, SOME GLUE AND A HOLE TOO)
127 SOMEWHERE IN MY MEMORY
126 SPECIAL GIFT
128 THE STAR CAROL
130 STILL, STILL, STILL
128 SUZY SNOWFLAKE
129 TENNESSEE CHRISTMAS
130 THAT CHRISTMAS FEELING
131 THIS CHRISTMAS
132 TOYLAND
132 THE TWELVE DAYS OF CHRISTMAS
133 UP ON THE HOUSETOP
133 WATCHMAN, TELL US OF THE NIGHT
134 WE NEED A LITTLE CHRISTMAS
135 WE THREE KINGS OF ORIENT ARE
135 WE WISH YOU A MERRY CHRISTMAS
136 WEXFORD CAROL
137 WHAT ARE YOU DOING NEW YEAR'S EVE?
136 WHAT CHILD IS THIS?
143 WHEN CHRISTMAS MORN IS DAWNING
144 WHEN SANTA CLAUS GETS YOUR LETTER
139 THE WHITE WORLD OF WINTER
138 WHO WOULD IMAGINE A KING
140 WONDERFUL CHRISTMASTIME
142 YOU DON'T HAVE TO BE ALONE
141 YOU'RE ALL I WANT FOR CHRISTMAS

# ALL I WANT FOR CHRISTMAS IS YOU

CLARINET



Words and Music by MARIAH CAREY
and WALTER AFANASIEFF

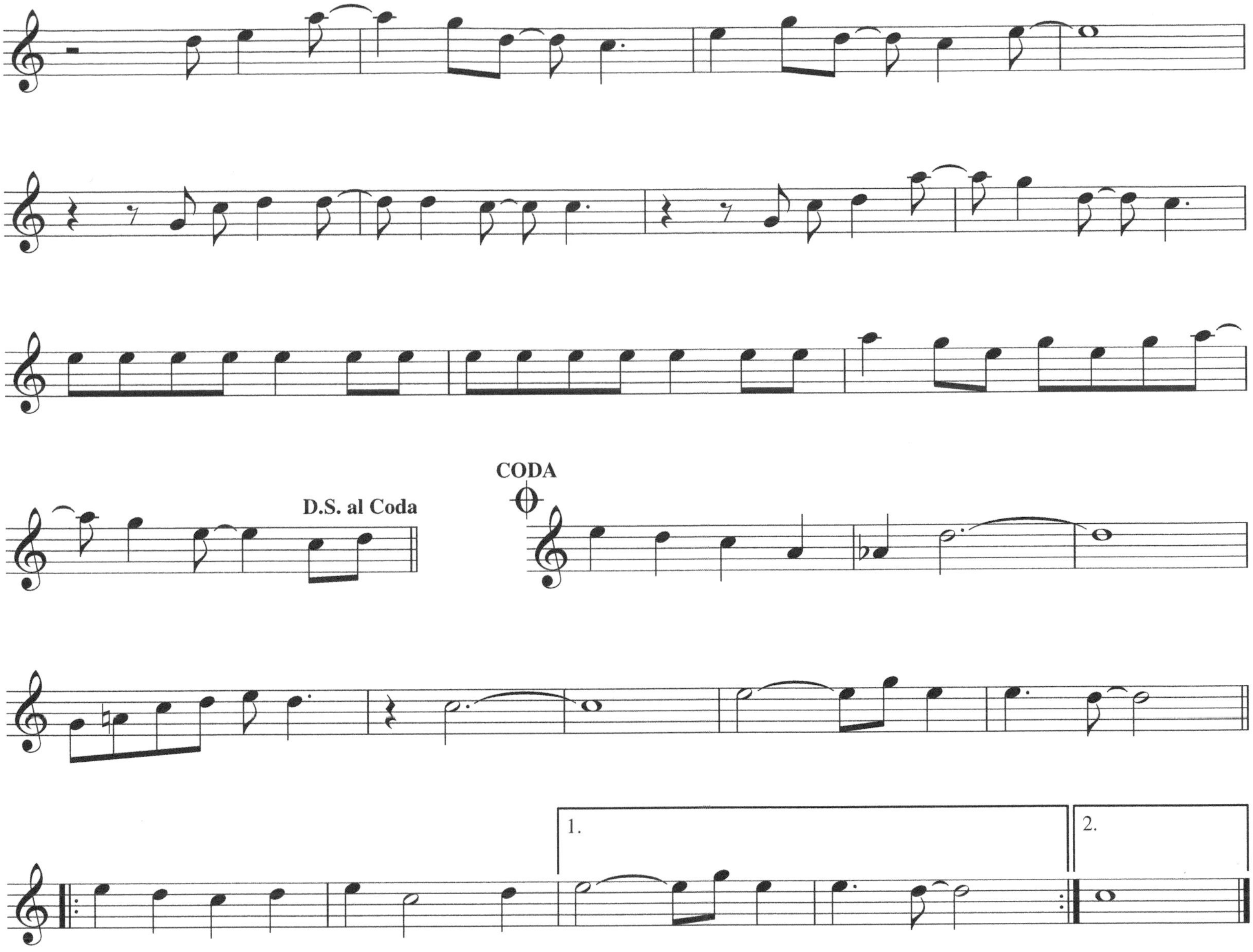


# A CAROLING WE GO



Music and Lyrics by
JOHNNY MARKS

**Moderately bright**

# ALL MY HEART THIS NIGHT REJOICES





Words and Music by JOHANN EBELING
and CATHERINE WINKWORTH

# ALL THROUGH THE NIGHT



Welsh Folksong

# ANGELS FROM THE REALMS OF GLORY

CLARINET



Words by JAMES MONTGOMERY
Music by HENRY T. SMART

# ANGELS WE HAVE HEARD ON HIGH



Traditional French Carol

# AS LONG AS THERE'S CHRISTMAS

from Walt Disney's BEAUTY AND THE BEAST - THE ENCHANTED CHRISTMAS

CLARINET



Music by RACHEL PORTMAN
Lyrics by DON BLACK

**Moderately**

# AS WITH GLADNESS MEN OF OLD

CLARINET



Words by WILLIAM CHATTERTON DIX
Music by CONRAD KOCHER

# AULD LANG SYNE



Words by ROBERT BURNS
Traditional Scottish Melody

# AWAY IN A MANGER



Traditional
Music by WILLIAM J. KIRKPATRICK

# BRAZILIAN SLEIGH BELLS

CLARINET



By PERCY FAITH

CLARINET

D.S. al Coda
CODA

# BABY, IT'S COLD OUTSIDE

from the Motion Picture NEPTUNE'S DAUGHTER

CLARINET



By FRANK LOESSER

1.
2.

# BECAUSE IT'S CHRISTMAS
## (For All the Children)

CLARINET



Music by BARRY MANILOW
Lyric by BRUCE SUSSMAN and JACK FELDMAN

# AWAY IN A MANGER



Traditional
Music by JAMES R. MURRAY

# BLUE CHRISTMAS

CLARINET



Words and Music by BILLY HAYES
and JAY JOHNSON

# BREAK FORTH, O BEAUTEOUS, HEAVENLY LIGHT



Words by JOHANN RIST
Melody by JOHANN SCHOP

# THE BOAR'S HEAD CAROL

CLARINET



Traditional English

# C-H-R-I-S-T-M-A-S



Words by JENNY LOU CARSON
Music by EDDY ARNOLD

# BRING A TORCH, JEANNETTE, ISABELLA

CLARINET



17th Century French Provençal Carol

# CAROL OF THE BELLS



Ukrainian Christmas Carol

# CAROL OF THE BIRDS



Traditional Catalonian Carol

# CAROLING, CAROLING

CLARINET



Words by WIHLA HUTSON
Music by ALFRED BURT

# THE CHIPMUNK SONG



Words and Music by
ROSS BAGDASARIAN

# A CHILD IS BORN IN BETHLEHEM



14th-Century Latin Text
Traditional Danish Melody

# CHRIST WAS BORN ON CHRISTMAS DAY



Traditional

# CHRISTMAS ALL ACROSS THE U.S.A.

CLARINET



Words and Music by
RITA ABRAMS

# CHRISTMAS IN DIXIE

CLARINET



Words and Music by JEFFREY COOK,
TEDDY GENTRY, MARK HERNDON
and RANDY OWEN

# CHRISTMAS IS ALL IN THE HEART

CLARINET



Words and Music by
STEVEN CURTIS CHAPMAN

To Coda
2
D.S. al Coda
(with repeat)
CODA
3

# CHRISTMAS IS

CLARINET



Lyrics by SPENCE MAXWELL
Music by PERCY FAITH

**Slowly**

# CHRISTMAS STAR

from the Twentieth Century Fox Feature Film HOME ALONE 2



Words by LESLIE BRICUSSE
Music by JOHN WILLIAMS

**Slowly, gently**

# CHRISTMAS TIME IS HERE

from A CHARLIE BROWN CHRISTMAS



Words by LEE MENDELSON
Music by VINCE GUARALDI

# CHRISTMAS IS A-COMIN'

## (May God Bless You)

CLARINET



Words and Music by
FRANK LUTHER

# THE CHRISTMAS SONG
## (Chestnuts Roasting on an Open Fire)

CLARINET



Music and Lyric by MEL TORME
and ROBERT WELLS

# COLD DECEMBER NIGHTS

CLARINET



Words and Music by MICHAEL McCARY
and SHAWN STOCKMAN

# THE CHRISTMAS WALTZ



Words by SAMMY CAHN
Music by JULE STYNE

**Moderately, with expression**

# COME, THOU LONG-EXPECTED JESUS

CLARINET



Words by CHARLES WESLEY
Music by ROWLAND HUGH PRICHARD

**Moderately**

# COVENTRY CAROL



Words by ROBERT CROO
Traditional English Melody

**Gently**

# DANCE OF THE SUGAR PLUM FAIRY

from THE NUTCRACKER

CLARINET



By PYOTR IL'YICH TCHAIKOVSKY

# DECK THE HALL



Traditional Welsh Carol

# DO THEY KNOW IT'S CHRISTMAS?

CLARINET



Words and Music by M. URE
and B. GELDOF

# DON'T SAVE IT ALL FOR CHRISTMAS DAY

CLARINET



Words and Music by CELINE DION, PETER ZIZZO and RIC WAKE

**Slowly in one, steadily**

2.
Slower

# DING DONG! MERRILY ON HIGH!





French Carol

# DO YOU HEAR WHAT I HEAR



Words and Music by NOEL REGNEY
and GLORIA SHAYNE

# FELIZ NAVIDAD



Music and Lyrics by
JOSÉ FELICIANO

# FROSTY THE SNOW MAN

CLARINET



Words and Music by STEVE NELSON
and JACK ROLLINS

**Moderately**

# THE FIRST NOEL

CLARINET



17th Century English Carol
Music from W. Sandys' *Christmas Carols*

# THE FRIENDLY BEASTS



Traditional English Carol

# FROM HEAVEN ABOVE TO EARTH I COME



Words and Music by
MARTIN LUTHER

# THE GIFT

CLARINET



Words and Music by TOM DOUGLAS
and JIM BRICKMAN

# GOING HOME FOR CHRISTMAS

CLARINET



Words and Music by STEVEN CURTIS CHAPMAN
and JAMES ISAAC ELLIOTT

**Rhythmically and flowing**

To Coda I
To Coda II
D.S. al Coda I
(take 2nd ending)
CODA I
D.S.S. al Coda II
CODA II

# FUM, FUM, FUM

CLARINET



Traditional Catalonian Carol

**Joyfully**

# GO, TELL IT ON THE MOUNTAIN



African-American Spiritual

**Moderately**

# GOD REST YE MERRY, GENTLEMEN

CLARINET



19th Century English Carol

**Brightly**

# GOOD CHRISTIAN MEN, REJOICE



14th Century Latin Text
14th Century German Melody

**Brightly**

# GOOD KING WENCESLAS



Words by JOHN M. NEALE
Music from *Piae Cantiones*

**Moderately**

# GRANDMA GOT RUN OVER BY A REINDEER

CLARINET



Words and Music by
RANDY BROOKS

# GRANDMA'S KILLER FRUITCAKE

CLARINET



Words and Music by ELMO SHROPSHIRE
and RITA ABRAMS

**Country Polka**

# THE GREATEST GIFT OF ALL

CLARINET



Words and Music by
JOHN JARVIS

# HARK! THE HERALD ANGELS SING



Words by CHARLES WESLEY
Music by FELIX MENDELSSOHN-BARTHOLDY

**Moderately**

# GROWN-UP CHRISTMAS LIST

CLARINET



Words and Music by DAVID FOSTER
and LINDA THOMPSON-JENNER

**Moderately slow**

# HE IS BORN, THE HOLY CHILD

(Il est ne, le Divin Enfant)



Traditional French Carol

# GREENWILLOW CHRISTMAS

CLARINET



By FRANK LOESSER

# HAPPY CHRISTMAS, LITTLE FRIEND



Lyrics by OSCAR HAMMERSTEIN II
Music by RICHARD RODGERS

1.
2.

# HAPPY HANUKKAH, MY FRIEND

(The Hanukkah Song)

CLARINET



Words and Music by JUSTIN WILDE
and DOUGLAS ALAN KONECKY

# HAPPY HOLIDAY

from the Motion Picture Irving Berlin's HOLIDAY INN



Words and Music by
IRVING BERLIN

# HARD CANDY CHRISTMAS

from THE BEST LITTLE WHOREHOUSE IN TEXAS

CLARINET



Words and Music by
CAROL HALL

# HE



Words by RICHARD MULLEN
Music by JACK RICHARDS

# HERE COMES SANTA CLAUS
(Right Down Santa Claus Lane)



Words and Music by GENE AUTRY
and OAKLEY HALDEMAN

**Moderately, in 2**

# HAPPY XMAS
## (War Is Over)

CLARINET



Words and Music by JOHN LENNON
and YOKO ONO

**Moderately**

# HERE WE COME A-WASSAILING

CLARINET



Traditional

# THE HOLLY AND THE IVY



18th Century English Carol

(There's No Place Like)
# HOME FOR THE HOLIDAYS

CLARINET



Words by AL STILLMAN
Music by ROBERT ALLEN

# HYMNE

CLARINET



By VANGELIS

# A HOLLY JOLLY CHRISTMAS

CLARINET



Music and Lyrics by
JOHNNY MARKS

# I AM SO GLAD ON CHRISTMAS EVE



Words by MARIE WEXELSEN
Music by PEDER KNUDSEN

# I HEARD THE BELLS ON CHRISTMAS DAY

CLARINET



Words by HENRY WADSWORTH LONGFELLOW
Music by JOHN BAPTISTE CALKIN

**Moderately slow**

# I HEARD THE BELLS ON CHRISTMAS DAY



Words by HENRY WADSWORTH LONGFELLOW
Adapted by JOHNNY MARKS
Music by JOHNNY MARKS

**Moderately**

# I SAW THREE SHIPS



Traditional English Carol

**Brightly**

# I SAW MOMMY KISSING SANTA CLAUS

CLARINET



Words and Music by
TOMMIE CONNOR

# I WONDER AS I WANDER



By JOHN JACOB NILES

# I'M SPENDING CHRISTMAS WITH YOU

CLARINET



Words and Music by
TOM OCCHIPINTI

# I'VE GOT MY LOVE TO KEEP ME WARM

from the 20th Century Fox Motion Picture ON THE AVENUE

CLARINET



Words and Music by
IRVING BERLIN

# I'LL BE HOME FOR CHRISTMAS

CLARINET



Words and Music by KIM GANNON
and WALTER KENT

# IN THE BLEAK MIDWINTER



Poem by CHRISTINA ROSSETTI
Music by GUSTAV HOLST

# IT MUST HAVE BEEN THE MISTLETOE

(Our First Christmas)

CLARINET



By JUSTIN WILDE
and DOUG KONECKY

# IT CAME UPON THE MIDNIGHT CLEAR



Words by EDMUND HAMILTON SEARS
Music by RICHARD STORRS WILLIS

# IT'S BEGINNING TO LOOK LIKE CHRISTMAS

CLARINET



By MEREDITH WILLSON

# IT'S JUST ANOTHER NEW YEAR'S EVE

CLARINET



Lyric by MARTY PANZER
Music by BARRY MANILOW

# IT'S CHRISTMAS TIME ALL OVER THE WORLD

CLARINET



Words and Music by
HUGH MARTIN

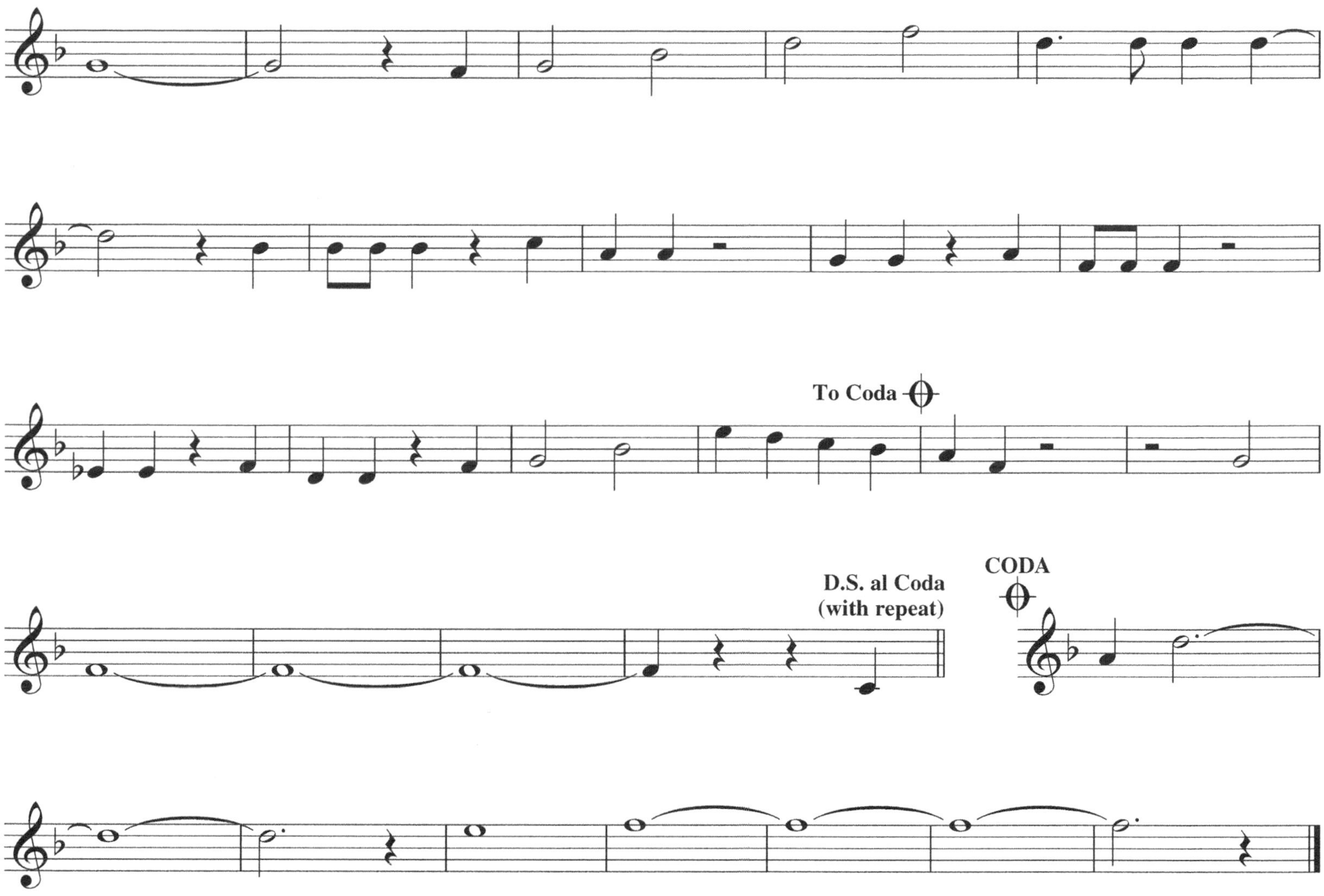


# JESUS HOLY, BORN SO LOWLY



Traditional Polish

# JESU, JOY OF MAN'S DESIRING

CLARINET



By JOHANN SEBASTIAN BACH

1.
2.

# JINGLE BELLS

CLARINET



Words and Music by
J. PIERPONT

# JINGLE, JINGLE, JINGLE



Music and Lyrics by
JOHNNY MARKS

# JOLLY OLD ST. NICHOLAS

Traditional 19th Century American Carol

# JINGLE-BELL ROCK

CLARINET



Words and Music by JOE BEAL
and JIM BOOTHE

**Moderately, with a Rock beat**

# LET'S HAVE AN OLD FASHIONED CHRISTMAS

CLARINET



Lyric by LARRY CONLEY
Music by JOE SOLOMON

# LAST CHRISTMAS

CLARINET



Words and Music by
GEORGE MICHAEL

# JOY TO THE WORLD



Words by ISAAC WATTS
Music by GEORGE FRIDERIC HANDEL

(Everybody's Waitin' For)

# THE MAN WITH THE BAG

CLARINET



Words and Music by HAROLD STANLEY,
IRVING TAYLOR and DUDLEY BROOKS

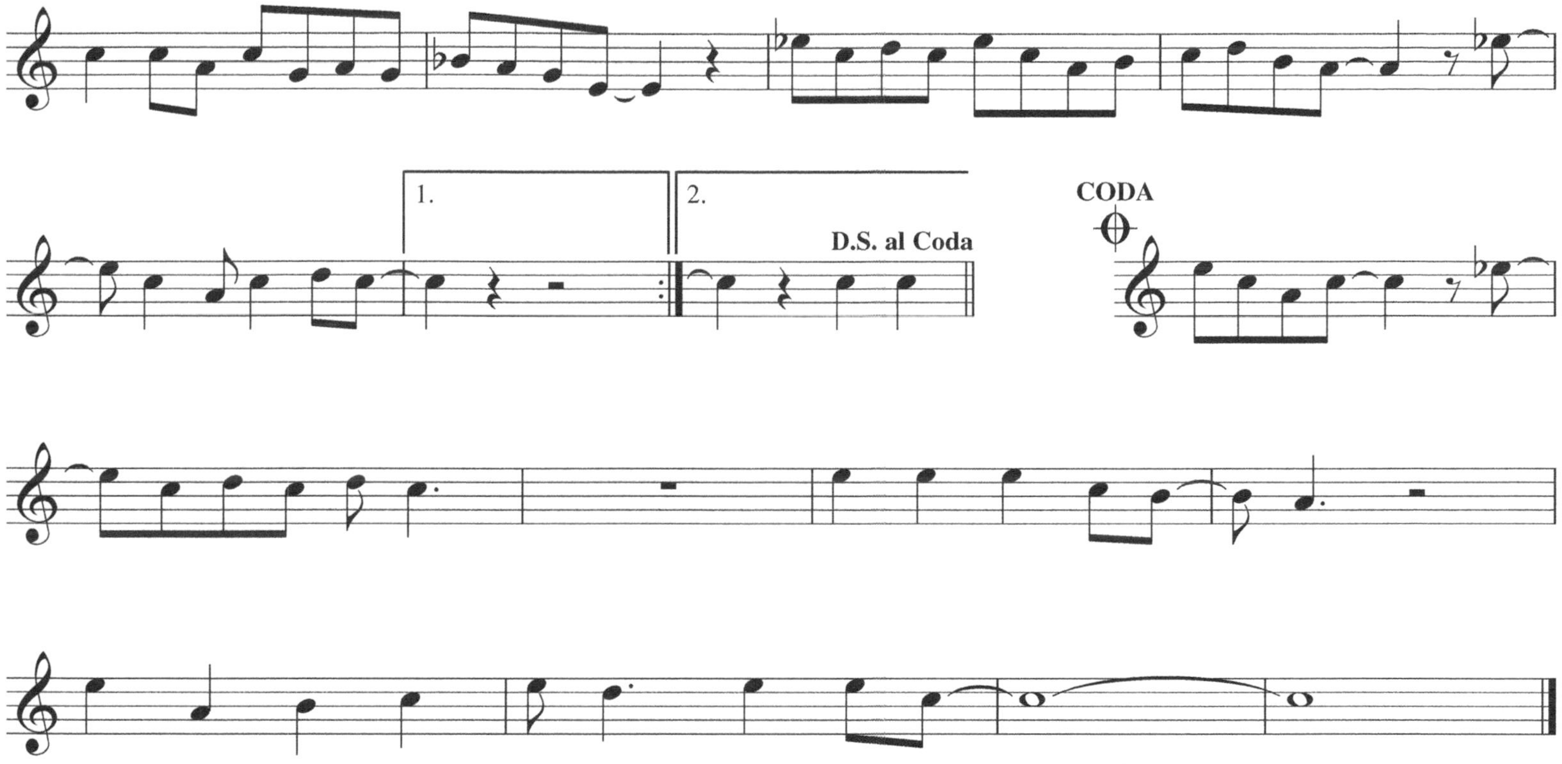


# LET IT SNOW! LET IT SNOW! LET IT SNOW!



Words by SAMMY CAHN
Music by JULE STYNE

# THE LAST MONTH OF THE YEAR

(What Month Was Jesus Born In?)

CLARINET



Words and Music by VERA HALL
Adapted and Arranged by RUBY PICKENS TARTT
and ALAN LOMAX

# LITTLE SAINT NICK



Words and Music by BRIAN WILSON
and MIKE LOVE

# LO, HOW A ROSE E'ER BLOOMING



15th Century German Carol
Music from *Alte Catholische Geistliche Kirchengesang*

# MARCH OF THE THREE KINGS

CLARINET



Words by M. L. HOHMAN
Traditional French Melody

# A MARSHMALLOW WORLD

CLARINET



Words by CARL SIGMAN
Music by PETER DE ROSE

# MASTERS IN THIS HALL

CLARINET



Traditional English

# MELE KALIKIMAKA



Words and Music by
ALEX ANDERSON

# MERRY CHRISTMAS, BABY

CLARINET



Words and Music by LOU BAXTER
and JOHNNY MOORE

**Blues tempo**

# MERRY CHRISTMAS, DARLING

CLARINET



Words and Music by RICHARD CARPENTER
and FRANK POOLER

# MERRY CHRISTMAS, MERRY CHRISTMAS

from the Twentieth Century Fox Feature Film HOME ALONE 2

CLARINET



Words by LESLIE BRICUSSE
Music by JOHN WILLIAMS

# MISS YOU MOST AT CHRISTMAS TIME

CLARINET



Words and Music by MARIAH CAREY
and WALTER AFANASIEFF

# THE MERRY CHRISTMAS POLKA



Words by PAUL FRANCIS WEBSTER
Music by SONNY BURKE

# MISTER SANTA

CLARINET



Words and Music by
PAT BALLARD

# A MERRY, MERRY CHRISTMAS TO YOU



Music and Lyrics by
JOHNNY MARKS

# MISTLETOE AND HOLLY



Words and Music by FRANK SINATRA,
DOK STANFORD and HENRY W. SANICOLA

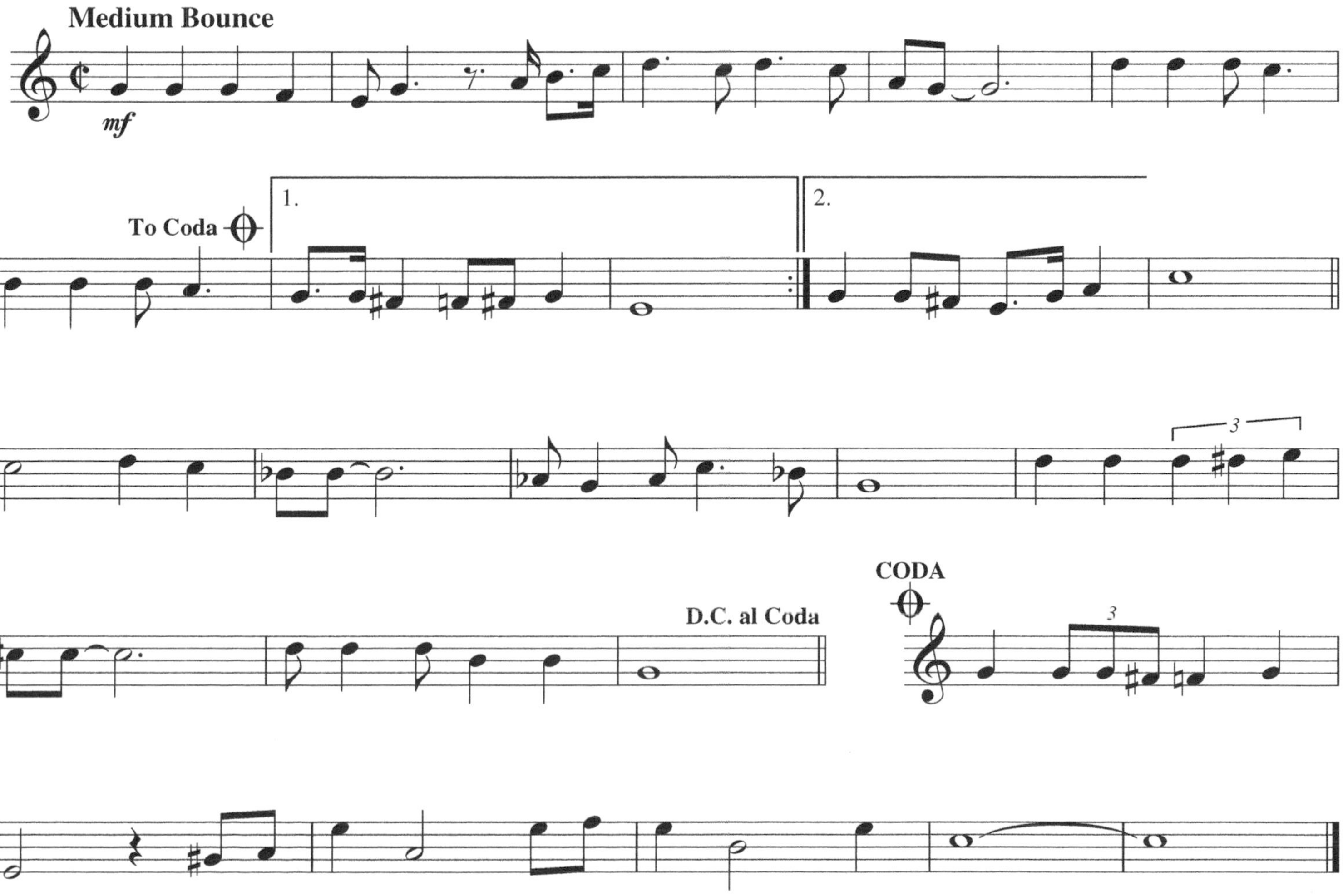

# THE MOST WONDERFUL DAY OF THE YEAR

CLARINET



Music and Lyrics by
JOHNNY MARKS

# THE NIGHT BEFORE CHRISTMAS SONG



Music by JOHNNY MARKS
Lyrics adapted by JOHNNY MARKS
from Clement Moore's Poem

# THE MOST WONDERFUL TIME OF THE YEAR

CLARINET



Words and Music by EDDIE POLA
and GEORGE WYLE

# MY FAVORITE THINGS

from THE SOUND OF MUSIC

CLARINET



Lyrics by OSCAR HAMMERSTEIN II
Music by RICHARD RODGERS

# MY ONLY WISH THIS YEAR

CLARINET



Words and Music by BRIAN KIERULF
and JOSHUA SCHWARTZ

# O CHRISTMAS TREE



Traditional German Carol

# O COME, ALL YE FAITHFUL

(Adeste Fideles)

CLARINET



Words and Music by JOHN FRANCIS WADE
Latin words translated by FREDERICK OAKELEY

**Moderately**

# NUTTIN' FOR CHRISTMAS



Words and Music by ROY BENNETT
and SID TEPPER

**Moderately bright**

# O COME, LITTLE CHILDREN



Words by C. VON SCHMIDT
Music by J.P.A. SCHULZ

**Quietly**

# O COME, O COME IMMANUEL

CLARINET



Plainsong, 13th Century

# O LITTLE TOWN OF BETHLEHEM



Words by PHILLIPS BROOKS
Music by LEWIS H. REDNER

# O SANCTISSIMA



Sicilian Carol

# O HOLY NIGHT

CLARINET



French words by PLACIDE CAPPEAU
English words by JOHN S. DWIGHT
Music by ADOLPHE ADAM

**Moderately**

# OF THE FATHER'S LOVE BEGOTTEN



Words by AURELIUS C. PRUDENTIUS
13th Century Plainsong

**Freely**

# ON CHRISTMAS NIGHT

CLARINET



Sussex Carol

# OLD TOY TRAINS



Words and Music by
ROGER MILLER

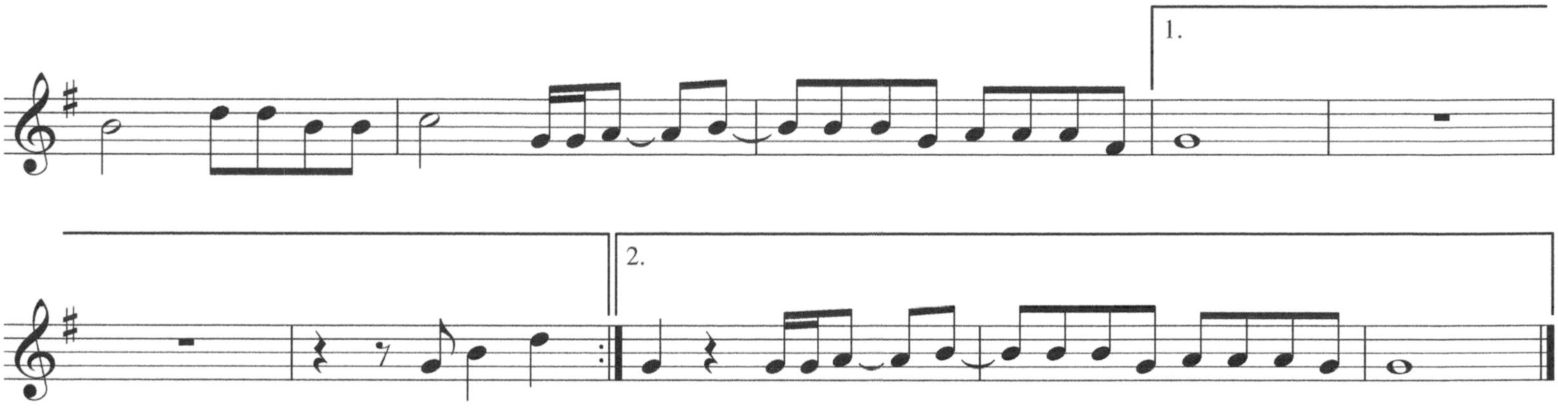


# PRETTY PAPER



Words and Music by
WILLIE NELSON

# PLEASE COME HOME FOR CHRISTMAS

CLARINET



Words and Music by CHARLES BROWN
and GENE REDD

# ONCE IN ROYAL DAVID'S CITY



Words by CECIL F. ALEXANDER
Music by HENRY J. GAUNTLETT

# PAT-A-PAN
## (Willie, Take Your Little Drum)

CLARINET



Words and Music by
BERNARD DE LA MONNOYE

# RISE UP, SHEPHERD, AND FOLLOW



African-American Spiritual

# ROCKIN' AROUND THE CHRISTMAS TREE

CLARINET



Music and Lyrics by
JOHNNY MARKS

# RUDOLPH THE RED-NOSED REINDEER

CLARINET



Music and Lyrics by
JOHNNY MARKS

# SANTA BABY

CLARINET



By JOAN JAVITS,
PHIL SPRINGER and TONY SPRINGER

# SANTA CLAUS IS BACK IN TOWN

CLARINET



Words and Music by JERRY LEIBER
and MIKE STOLLER

**Slow Blues tempo**

# SANTA CLAUS IS COMIN' TO TOWN



Words by HAVEN GILLESPIE
Music by J. FRED COOTS

**Moderate Swing** (♫ = ♩ 3 ♪)

# SHAKE ME I RATTLE
## (Squeeze Me I Cry)



Words and Music by HAL HACKADY
and CHARLES NAYLOR

# SANTA, BRING MY BABY BACK

(To Me)

CLARINET



Words and Music by CLAUDE DeMETRUIS
and AARON SCHROEDER

# SHEPHERDS, SHAKE OFF YOUR DROWSY SLEEP

CLARINET



Traditional French Carol

# SILVER AND GOLD



Music and Lyrics by
JOHNNY MARKS

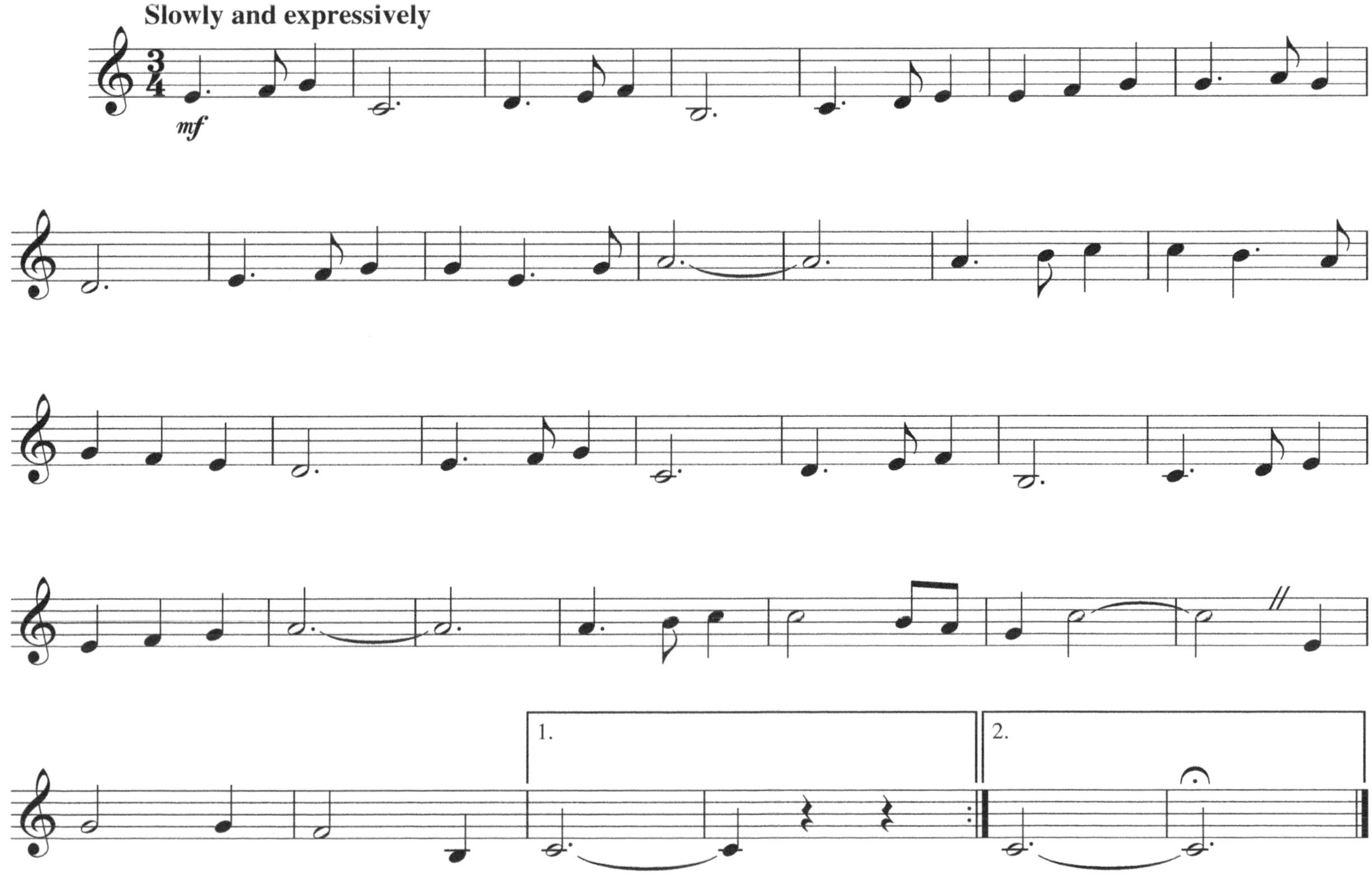

# SILENT NIGHT

CLARINET



Words by JOSEPH MOHR
Translated by JOHN F. YOUNG
Music by FRANZ X. GRUBER

# SILVER BELLS

from the Paramount Picture THE LEMON DROP KID



Words and Music by JAY LIVINGSTON
and RAY EVANS

# SING WE NOW OF CHRISTMAS

CLARINET



Traditional French Carol

# SNOWFALL



Lyrics by RUTH THORNHILL
Music by CLAUDE THORNHILL

# SOME THINGS FOR CHRISTMAS

## (A Snake, Some Mice, Some Glue and a Hole Too)

CLARINET



Lyric by JACQUELYN REINACH and JOAN LAMPORT
Music by JACQUELYN REINACH

**Moderate Waltz tempo**

# SOME CHILDREN SEE HIM



Lyric by WIHLA HUTSON
Music by ALFRED BURT

# SPECIAL GIFT

CLARINET



Words and Music by MYRON DAVIS
and STANLEY BROWN

# SOMEWHERE IN MY MEMORY

from the Twentieth Century Fox Motion Picture HOME ALONE



Words by LESLIE BRICUSSE
Music by JOHN WILLIAMS

**Gently and with simplicity**

# THE STAR CAROL

CLARINET



Lyric by WIHLA HUTSON
Music by ALFRED BURT

**Tenderly, with much expression**

# SUZY SNOWFLAKE



Words and Music by SID TEPPER
and ROY BENNETT

**Moderately**

# TENNESSEE CHRISTMAS

CLARINET



Words and Music by AMY GRANT
and GARY CHAPMAN

# STILL, STILL, STILL

CLARINET



Salzburg Melody, c.1819
Traditional Austrian Text

# THAT CHRISTMAS FEELING



Words and Music by BENNIE BENJAMIN
and GEORGE WEISS

# THIS CHRISTMAS

CLARINET



Words and Music by DONNY HATHAWAY
and NADINE McKINNOR

# TOYLAND

CLARINET



Words by GLEN MacDONOUGH
Music by VICTOR HERBERT

# THE TWELVE DAYS OF CHRISTMAS



Traditional English Carol

**These bars are played a different number of times for each verse.*

# UP ON THE HOUSETOP

CLARINET



Words and Music by
B.R. HANDY

# WATCHMAN, TELL US OF THE NIGHT



Traditional

# WE NEED A LITTLE CHRISTMAS

from MAME

CLARINET



Music and Lyric by
JERRY HERMAN

# WE THREE KINGS OF ORIENT ARE

CLARINET



Words and Music by
JOHN H. HOPKINS, JR.

# WE WISH YOU A MERRY CHRISTMAS



Traditional English Folksong

# WEXFORD CAROL





Traditional Irish Carol

# WHAT CHILD IS THIS?



Words by WILLIAM C. DIX
16th Century English Melody

# WHAT ARE YOU DOING NEW YEAR'S EVE?

CLARINET



By FRANK LOESSER

# WHO WOULD IMAGINE A KING

from the Touchstone Motion Picture THE PREACHER'S WIFE

CLARINET



Words and Music by MERVYN WARREN
and HALLERIN HILTON HILL

# THE WHITE WORLD OF WINTER



Words by MITCHELL PARISH
Music by HOAGY CARMICHAEL

**Moderately, with a lift**

# WONDERFUL CHRISTMASTIME

CLARINET



Words and Music by
PAUL McCARTNEY

# YOU'RE ALL I WANT FOR CHRISTMAS



Words and Music by GLEN MOORE
and SEGER ELLIS

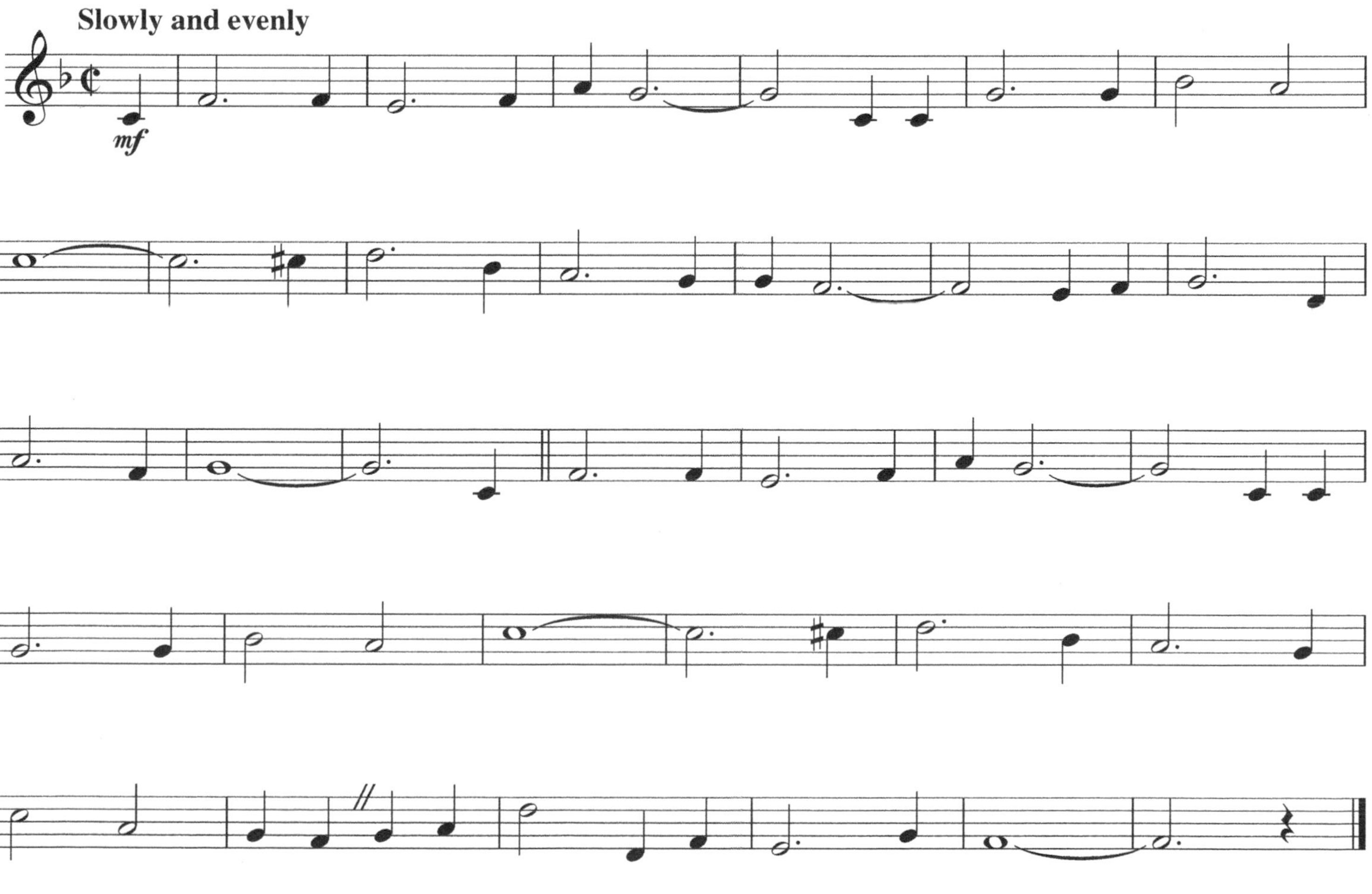

# YOU DON'T HAVE TO BE ALONE

CLARINET



Words and Music by VEIT RENN,
JOSHUA CHASEZ and DAVID NICOLL

# WHEN CHRISTMAS MORN IS DAWNING



Traditional Swedish

# WHEN SANTA CLAUS GETS YOUR LETTER

CLARINET



Music and Lyrics by
JOHNNY MARKS